# PASSENGER CARS OF NEW ENGLAND

## VOLUME 2

## BANGOR & AROOSTOOK AND MAINE CENTRAL

BY

ROBERT A. LILJESTRAND

&

DAVID R. SWEETLAND

All of the photographs in this book are available from...

Bob's Photo
37 Spring St.
Ansonia, CT 06401

1-203-734-6666

## The Railroad Press

The Railroad Press
PO Box 444
Hanover, PA 17331-0444

Copyright © 2000 by The Railroad Press. All rights reserved. No part of this book may be reproduced in part or whole, in any form or means whatsoever, without written permission from the publisher, except for brief quotations used in reviews.

Printed in the United States of America.

International Standard Book Number 0-9657709-8-2

*The Railroad Press*
Publishers of:

*TRP Magazine*

*1930's New England Steam Action: Worcester*

*Passenger Cars of New England Volume 1: B&M*

*Altoona Action*

*ALCO Reference #1*

*ALCO's to Allentown*

# CONTENTS

| BAR | | MEC | |
|---|---|---|---|
| Introduction | 3 | Introduction | 28 |
| Business Car | 5 | Wooden Coaches | 30 |
| Dining Cars | 6 | Steel Coaches | 34 |
| Wooden Coaches | 8 | RPO-Baggage | 38 |
| Steel Coach | 16 | Baggage Cars | 40 |
| Combines | 17 | Combines | 41 |
| Baggage Cars | 22 | Motor Coaches | 44 |
| RPO-Baggage | 25 | Work Cars | 45 |
| Work Cars | 26 | Office Cars | 48 |

# DEDICATION

### Sue Sweetland

This book is dedicated to my wife, Sue, who has helped me edit railroad books for over ten years. Sue is a native of the state of Maine, originally lived in Wilton in the heart of Maine Central territory and is a graduate of the University of Maine.

# ACKNOWLEDGEMENTS

This book is based on the collection of black and white negatives owned by Robert A. Liljestrand. Copies of the photographs can be obtained through Bob's Photo, 37 Spring Street, Ansonia, CT, 06401. Text and captions were written by David R. Sweetland. This is not a complete list of all passenger cars owned by the BAR and MEC.

A special thanks to George Melvin, former employee of the Maine Central and rail historian for technical assistance on passenger equipment and editing of the book. Also to Janet S. Watson for word processing the text and J. Emmon Lancaster and Russ Monroe for the loan of additional Maine Central photographs.

---

Front Cover Photos: BAR business car #100 stood on a cold day in February 1959 at Northern Maine Junction. Riding on black six-wheel trucks, the car was built by the Pullman Company in 1928. Its all light gray carbody had a wide dark blue center stripe and trucks, steps and underframe painted black.

Maine Central wooden combine #502 stopped at the Bangor Station in January 1959. Built by Laconia Car Company in 1910, it had a red wooden carbody with a truss-rod underframe, a black roof and five-inch gold leaf lettering for the Maine Central under the windows at the center line of the car.

Rear Cover Photos: BAR RPO-Baggage Car #566 photographic location was the Bangor Station in October 1955. The BAR owned four of the unique "American Flyer" head end cars with a 15-foot mail section. During the mid to late 1950s, these cars were painted with a light gray carbody, a dark blue center stripe and dark blue Bangor & Aroostook lettering near the roof line.

Maine Central coach #218 was parked on the Bangor Station storage track in October 1958. Painting arrangement included a dark green carbody with black roof, trucks and underframe, and five inch gold leaf lettering and numbers centered under the windows. (All color cover photos by David R. Sweetland)

# INTRODUCTION

## Bangor & Aroostook Passenger Equipment

Chartered in 1891, the Bangor & Aroostook operated a 602-mile railroad by 1950. Passenger revenue for 1950 was $370,131 with an overall operating ratio of 69% for both passenger and freight service. At this mid-century mark, the BAR operated two principal passenger trains, AROOSTOOK FLYER and POTATOLAND and four branch-line locals.

Up until 1935, the Bangor & Aroostook had a fleet of very old wooden coaches, combines and baggage cars being purchased in small groups around the turn of the century. Its most modern passenger-carrying car was business car #100, built by the Pullman Company in 1928. By 1950, its passenger car fleet was down to twenty-one coaches, twelve combination baggage-coaches, three dining cars and seventeen other head-end cars.

After coming out of the Great Depression, the BAR ordered two new 4-8-2s, #107 - 108, from Alco in 1935 and a group of modern 2-8-0s, #400 - 404. The railroad's management also focused on its passenger car fleet. After looking at "American Flyer" cars ordered by Boston and Maine and New Haven, the BAR ordered (lot W6521) three thirty-six seat lounge - twenty-four seat coach and dinette cars, #150 - 152, for delivery between July and October 1937. Also included in the order were two (lot W6522) eighty-four seat coaches, #230 - 321, and three (lot W6520) RPO-baggage cars, #566 - 568. No other railroad in the US or Canada ordered "American Flyer" styled head-end cars. Built at the Osgood-Bradley Plant of Pullman - Standard in Worcester, Massachusetts, BAR #566 - 568 had a fifteen-foot postal section and the rest a baggage car with two five-foot sliding doors per side. Like the B&M, the passenger cars did not have side skirts and rode on 41-E trucks. A repeat order (lot W6560) was placed by the BAR for one more baggage-mail car #569 for delivery in June 1938. Painted a dark green, the color scheme was changed to gray with a wide blue stripe after delivery of diesel units. The cars supplemented a fleet of forty-eight wooden coaches and combines built between 1893 and 1910. With the delivery of these cars, the AROOSTOOK FLYER was introduced in August 1937 powered by Pacifics. One steel baggage car, #531, was added in 1946.

The Bangor and Aroostook's next order (lot W6882) for three coaches, #250 KATAHDIN, #251 CHIPPEWA and #252 MOHAWK was placed with Pullman - Standard in November 1948 at about the same time the road ordered two E-7, #700 - 701 passenger diesels from EMD joining two steam-equipped F-3s, #506 - 507 purchased in May 1948. Bangor & Aroostook's first diesel passenger train (Train #7) took place on May 14, 1948. Delivered in August 1949, these cars went into service on the POTATOLAND SPECIAL and AROOSTOOK FLYER between Bangor and Van Buren, Maine, a 235-mile run. The three cars cost $325,500 with annual $50,000 payments made until October 1956.

In April 1953, the Bangor & Aroostook added to a New Haven order (lot W6942) for two six-section, six-roomette, four double-bedroom sleeping cars. Delivered in late 1964/early 1955, these two sleepers, #80 NORTH TWIN LAKE and #81 SOUTH TWIN LAKE were for Pullman service from Van Buren via Train #8 to Bangor and connecting service via the Maine Central & Boston & Maine to Boston. Returning from Boston on the GULL, the sleeper connected with BAR Train #1 at Bangor and ended at Van Buren. It is interesting that the BAR had no spares for these two sleepers on their 1000 mile round-trip assignments.

After the end of operation for the AROOSTOOK FLYER in 1957, cars #250 - 252 were sold to the Ontario Northland in 1959 and in 1965 Pullman sleepers #80 and 81 went to the Canadian National. The BAR closed its door on passenger service on September 4, 1961, when Trains #2 and 9 made their last runs.

# Bangor & Aroostook
# Passenger Car Roster   1925 - 1957 *

| Number | Builder | Date | Type | Notes |
|---|---|---|---|---|
| 80 - 81 | PS | 1955 | Sleeper | Steel |
| 100 | PS | 1928 | Business | Steel |
| 150 - 152 | PS | 1937 | Buffet-Lounge | Steel |
| 194 - 196 | | | Parlor-Café | Wood - steel underframe |
| 200 | | | Business | |
| 202 - 207 | | | Coach | Wood - open platform |
| 209 - 214 | | | Coach | Wood - steel underframe |
| 218 - 224 | | | Coach | Wood - steel underframe |
| 230 - 231 | PS | 1937 | Coach | Steel |
| 250 - 253 | PS | 1949 | Coach | Steel |
| 301 | | | Coach | Wood - open platform |
| 305 - 311 | | | Coach | Wood - steel underframe |
| 313 - 315 | | | Coach | Wood - steel underframe |
| 401 - 403 | | | Combine | Wood - open platform |
| 405 - 408 | | | Combine | Wood - open platform |
| 450 - 454 | | | Combine | Wood - open platform |
| 455 | | | Combine | Wood |
| 477 - 478 | | | Coach | Wood |
| 480 - 481 | | | Coach | Wood |
| 483 | | | Coach | Wood |
| 500 - 529 | various | | | Baggage   Wood |
| 506 - 508 | | | Baggage | Wood - steel underframe |
| 530 | | | Baggage | Steel |
| 531 | | 1946 | Baggage | Steel |
| 532 | | | Baggage | Steel |
| 564 - 565 | | | Baggage-Mail | Steel - 15 foot RPO |
| 566 - 568 | PS | 1937 | Baggage-Mail | Steel - 15 foot RPO |
| 569 | PS | 1938 | Baggage-Mail | Steel - 15 foot RPO |
| 570 | | 1927 | Baggage-Mail | Steel - 30 foot RPO ex C&O 68 |
| 600 | | 1910 | Combine | Wood - steel underframe ex C69 |
| 601 | | 1929 | Baggage-Mail | Steel - 15 foot RPO |

\* Based on the 1943 Official Register of Passenger Train Equipment and
   the December 1956 BAR Passenger Car Diagrams

# BUSINESS CAR

Bangor & Aroostook business car #100, originally ITSUITSME, was built by the Pullman Company in November 1928, lot 6176 plan 7205. This all-steel open-platform office car has three state rooms, a dining section, a kitchen/pantry, servants quarters and an observation room. Riding on Pullman 6-wheel trucks, #100 was photographed at the Derby Shops on July 24, 1968. In the blue and gray color scheme, #100 was at Northern Maine Junction on August 8, 1959.

# DINING CARS

Bangor & Aroostook started a passenger train modernization program in 1937 when it took delivery of two eighty-four-seat coaches, three thirty-six-seat coach dinettes and three RPO baggage cars, all of the so-called "American Flyer" design. Coach-dinette cars #150 - 152 were delivered from the Osgood-Bradley plant of Pullman - Standard in July through October 1937. The cars rode on 41-E friction bearing trucks and the car-body had no side skirts. These eighty-four foot, six and one quarter inch long cars had seating for twenty-four in the coach portion, thirty-six in the lounge-dining area and a small galley/kitchen. On July 19, 1952, #152 was at Caribou, Maine, in a passenger train.

Wooden dining car #195 rode on Pullman 6-wheel trucks, had truss rods and a steel underframe applied before 1926. On the dining room end, the car had a full vestibule, but on the kitchen end, there was only a one-half a vestibule. Coupled to a battery charger, #195 waited at Derby, Maine, on July 16, 1935.

Parlor café car #196 was actually an open-platform observation riding on Pullman six-wheel trucks and a truss-rod underframe. Steel plating had been applied above the windows, but below the belt rail the wooden siding was still exposed. In July 1937, #196 was at Van Buren, Maine, at the rear of a passenger train.

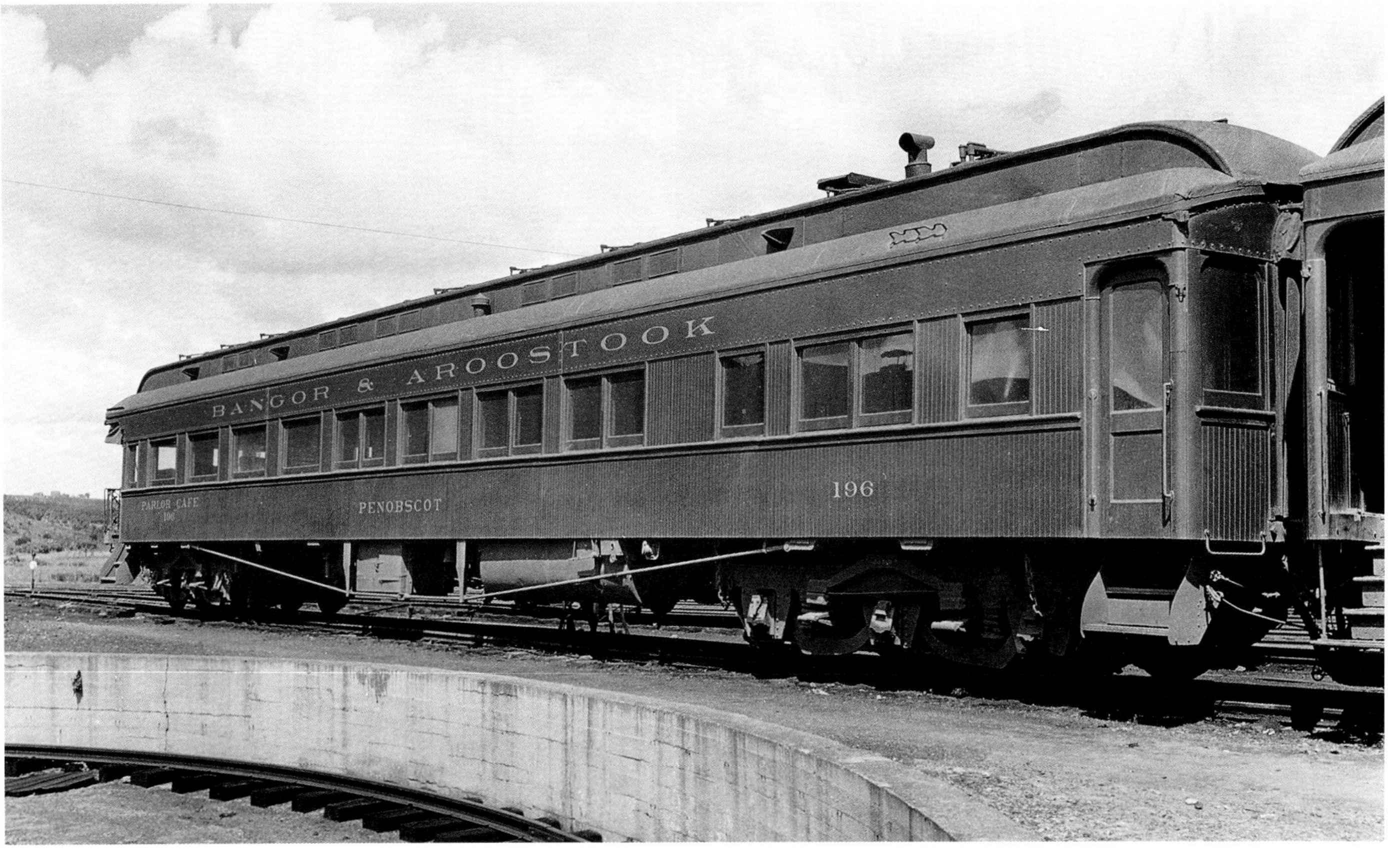

# WOODEN COACHES

Open-platform wooden coach #202 was placed at Derby, Maine, on July 16, 1935. Heated by two stoves, #202 seated about seventy-two passengers. Built on a truss-rod underframe, the coach rode on four-wheel drop-equalized trucks. Due to the age of the car, one end platform and steps were sagging.

Wooden coach #209 had a semi-closed vestibule and eight paired windows plus two single windows per side. Safety chains were still in place between the four-wheel drop-equalized trucks and carbody. Coupled to a wooden caboose, #209 was at Van Buren, Maine, in July 1937.

With stained glass windows in the upper sash, coach #210 waited at Northern Maine Junction on July 17, 1937, near the coaling tower. Its wooden carbody ended with a semi-closed vestibule and cast iron grills on either side of the diaphragm. Safety chains were provided on either side of the coupler and a flexible rubber steam connector hung under the coupler.

At the Bangor Station in July 1935, coach #212 was coupled to RPO #563 on the storage track. Coach #212 had a seating capacity of sixty-eight passengers in an under 70-foot long coach. This semi-closed vestibule coach had a truss-rod underframe and four-wheel drop-equalized trucks with an electrical system installed for lighting after the car was built.

Closed vestibule wooden coach #220 was at Van Buren, Maine, in July 1937 coupled to other passenger equipment. Each side had ten paired windows for a seating capacity of eighty-four passengers. A washroom with dry toilet installed had been installed at the far end. The truss-rod wooden carbody rode on four-wheel drop-equalized trucks with plain bearings.

On the storage tracks at Bangor Station in July 1935 was closed-vestibule coach #224. Seating eighty-four passengers, the wooden coach had a truss-rod underframe and four-wheel drop-equalized trucks. A view of the underframe disclosed a generator, battery box and standby plug for the electrical system. Ten paired windows covered the passenger section of the coach.

Wooden open-platform coach #301 was coupled to another open platform coach at Caribou, Maine, in July 1937. Its four-wheel trucks had special cast-steel equalizers and outside hanger-type brake beams. Coal stoves provided heat for passengers at opposite ends of the car for this coach-smoker. Screens were provided at five window locations along each side for summertime air circulation.

Semi-closed vestibule coach #305 waited at Derby, Maine, on July 17, 1935, coupled between a coach and baggage car. These semi-closed vestibules cars provided passengers some protection when crossing between cars, especially during the Maine winters. The coach had eight paired windows for the passengers plus single glass windows at each end. On the near end of #305, the frosted glass window covered the washroom with dry toilet.

The #305-309 group of cars looked very much the same with a truss-rod underframe, eight paired windows per side and drop-equalized trucks. Screens were provided at the end paired windows for summertime air circulation. Electric lights had not been installed in this car at the time of this photograph at Derby on July 17, 1935.

BAR coach #308 was at the Bangor Station in July 1937. This eight paired-window coach had electric lighting installed as indicated by the roof wiring, underbody generator standby plug-in receptacle, and battery boxes. The truss-rod underframe was deeper than that on the #305-306 group of passenger cars.

Narrow vestibule coach #309 waited on the passenger car storage track at Bangor in July 1935. The wooden coach with a truss-rod underframe rode on four-wheel drop-equalized trucks. The cast iron ornamental trim on the narrow vestibule, top and bottom, was still in place. Of all the side windows, only two had window screens.

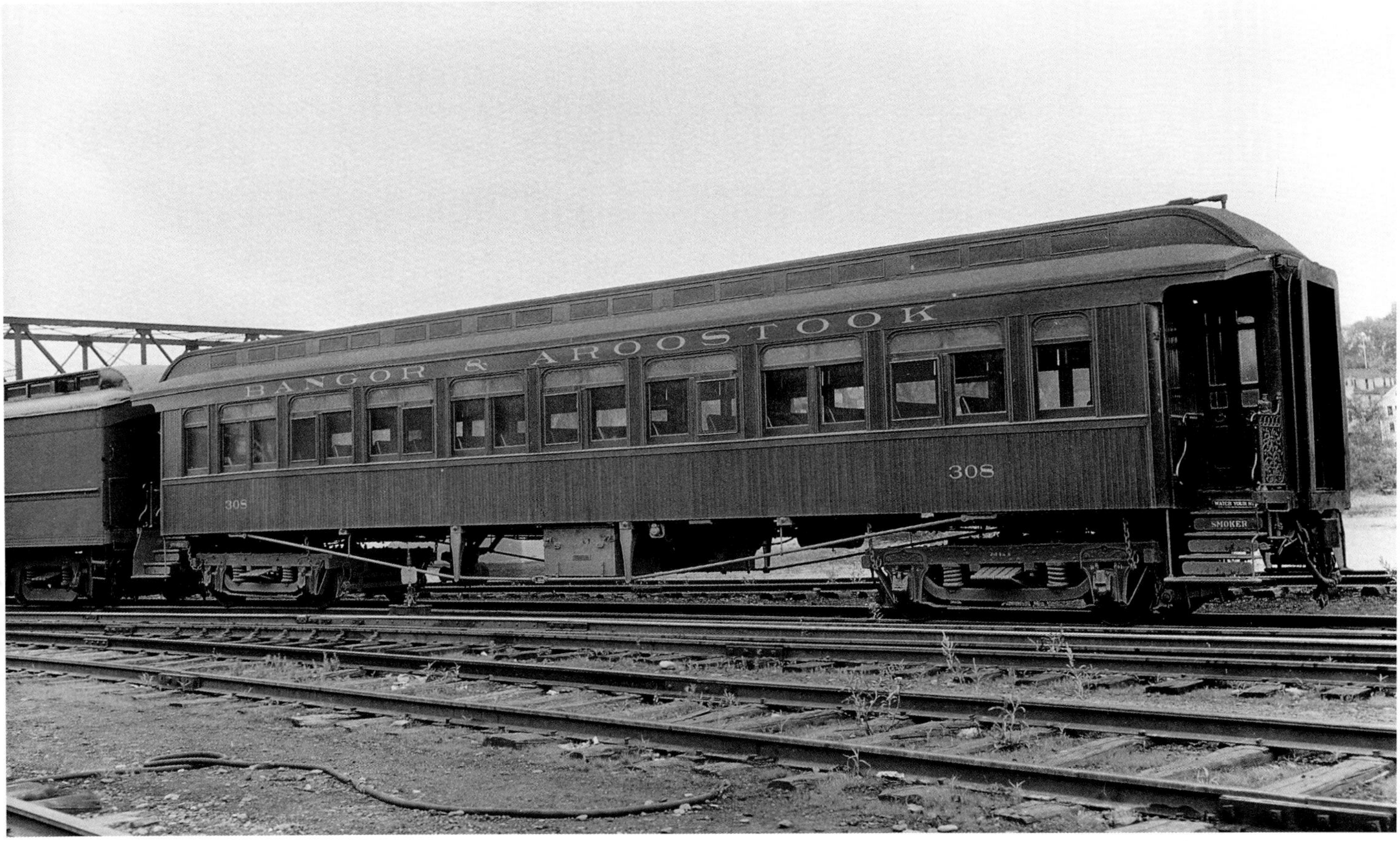

Volume 2  Bangor & Aroostook / Maine Central

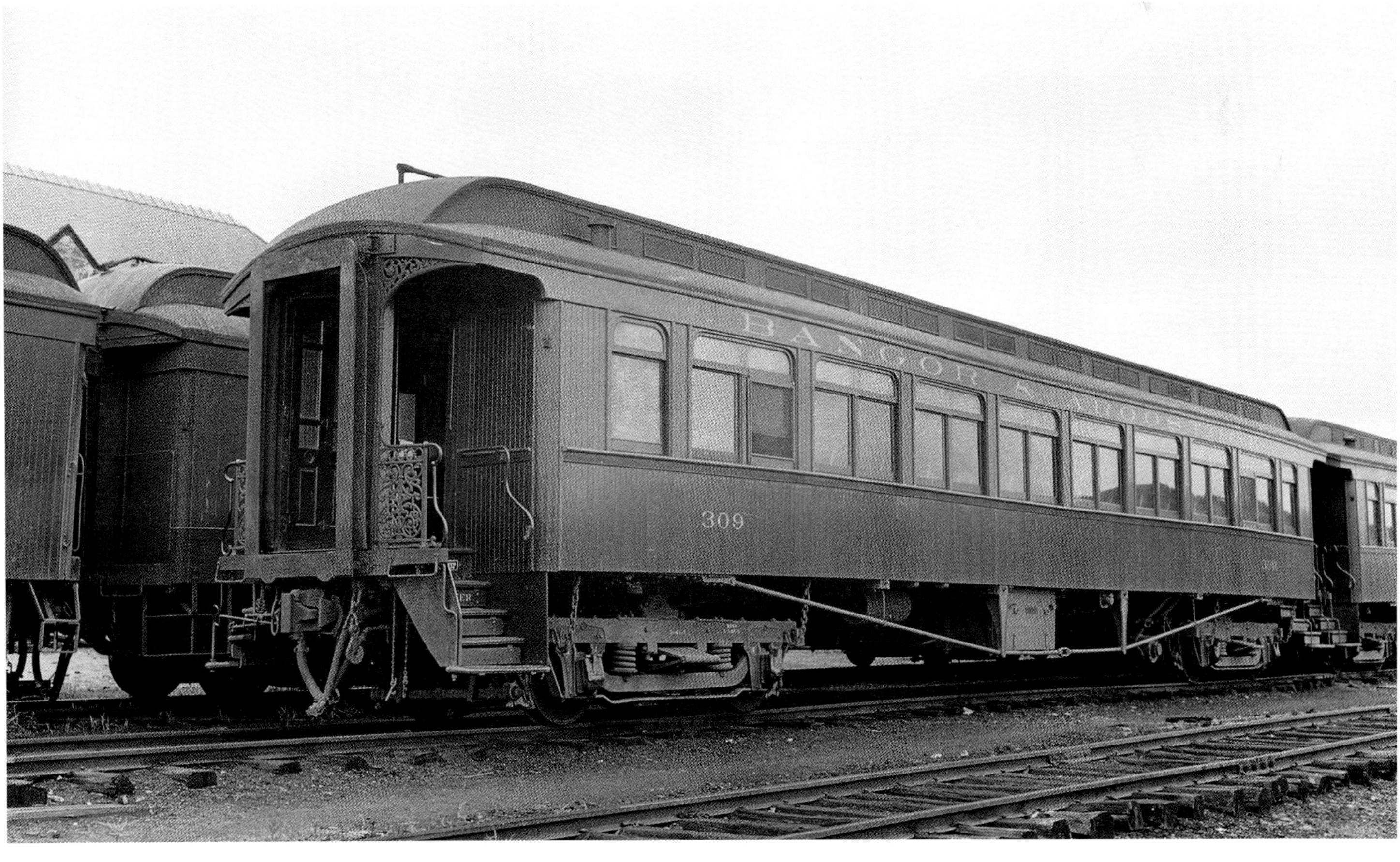

PASSENGER CARS OF NEW ENGLAND

BAR coach #310 was in the lineup at Bangor station on July 17, 1935. A little newer car than #309, #310 rode on newer style drop-equalized plain-bearing trucks and had a steel underframe. Eight paired windows plus one single window at the seats provided seating for sixty-eight passengers. The upper windowpane had rounded corners and two windows were equipped with screens. This sixty-five foot three-inch long coach seated sixty-six.

BAR coach #314 was at Van Buren, Maine, in July 1937 coupled to RPO-baggage #563. The narrow-vestibule doors were in the closed position and all windows were closed including the five with screens. At a later shopping, the upper windowpanes would be covered to give the car a more modern look. Coach #314 had a complete steel underframe, measured sixty-five foot three-inches overall and seated sixty-eight passengers.

Coaches #314 and 315 were two similar cars, both with the upper window panes now covered. These narrow-vestibule cars with four-wheel drop-equalizer trucks had steel underframes. Looking under the carbody, one can see the lighting generator, brake beam safety straps and truck safety chains connected to the side sills. Coach #315 was at Van Buren, Maine, on July 19, 1952. Car dimensions and seating were the same as #314, but this car seated 70 passengers. Wooden cars 310, 314 and 315 with steel underframes lasted into the early 1950s.

# STEEL COACH

In the summer of 1937, the BAR took delivery of two, #230-231, eighty-four seat coaches from Pullman-Standard. Built at the Osgood-Bradley Plant in Worcester, these "American Flyer" steel coaches rode on four-wheel 41-E trucks with plain bearings. As opposed to the New Haven, these cars did not have side skirts and came in the ten-window arrangement. Coupled to Caboose #C-42, coach #231 was on a special train at Madawaska, Maine, on July 19, 1952. In 1962, #231 was sold to the Maine Central and rebuilt to Maintenance of Way crew car #902.

Wooden combine #403 rode on four-wheel friction-bearing trucks and had a truss-rod underframe. For this open-platform baggage-coach, the baggage section extended two windows into the coach area and a coal stove provided heat for the passengers. On a storage track, #403 was photographed in August 1948. Seating for thirty-four was provided in the coach section.

Open-platform combine #405 was coupled to coach #301 at Caribou, Maine, in July 1937. Originally the wooden combine had only one window in the baggage section, but the baggage compartment had been expanded to cover two windows of the original passenger section. This non-electrified combine rode on four-wheel drop-equalized trucks, had a truss-rod underframe and carried thirty-two seated passengers.

# COMBINE

BANGOR & AROOSTOOK
BAGGAGE
403
403

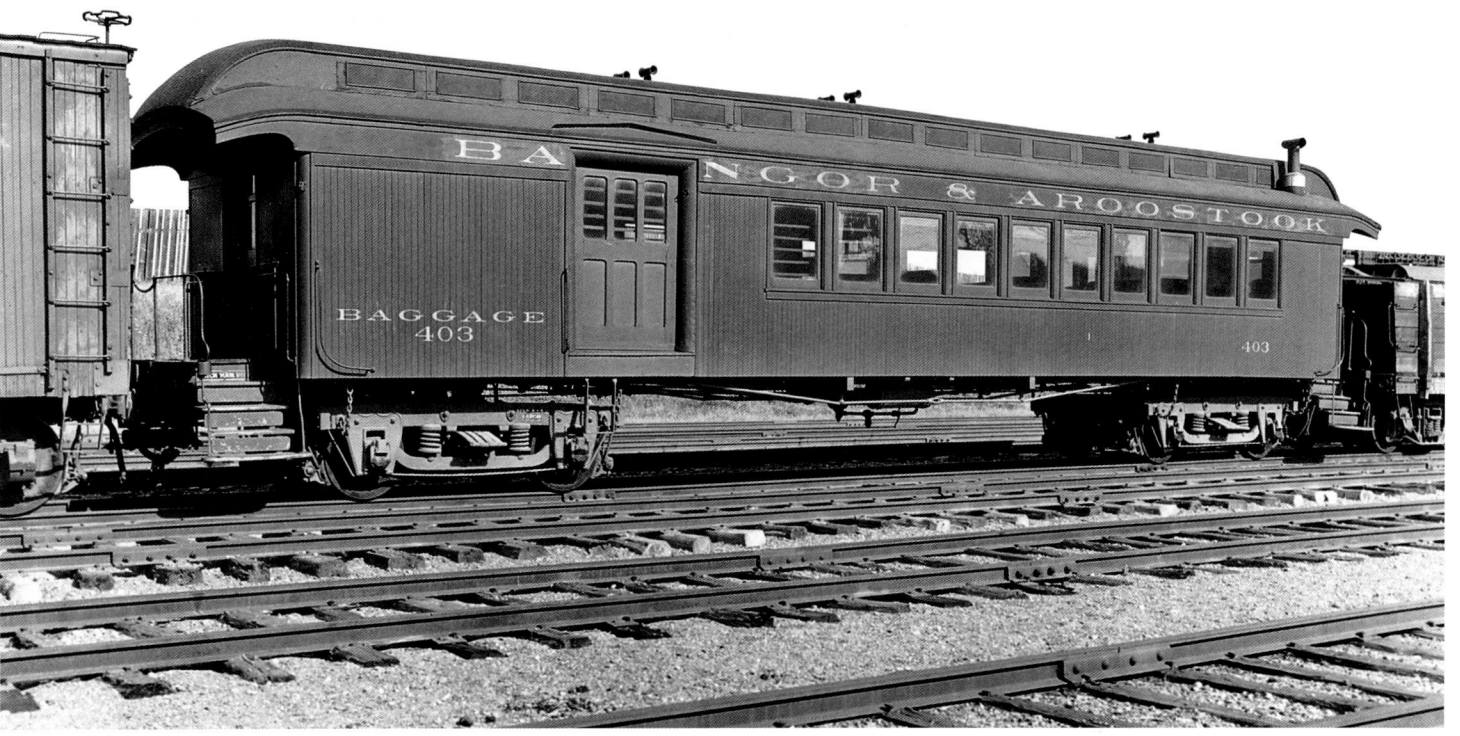

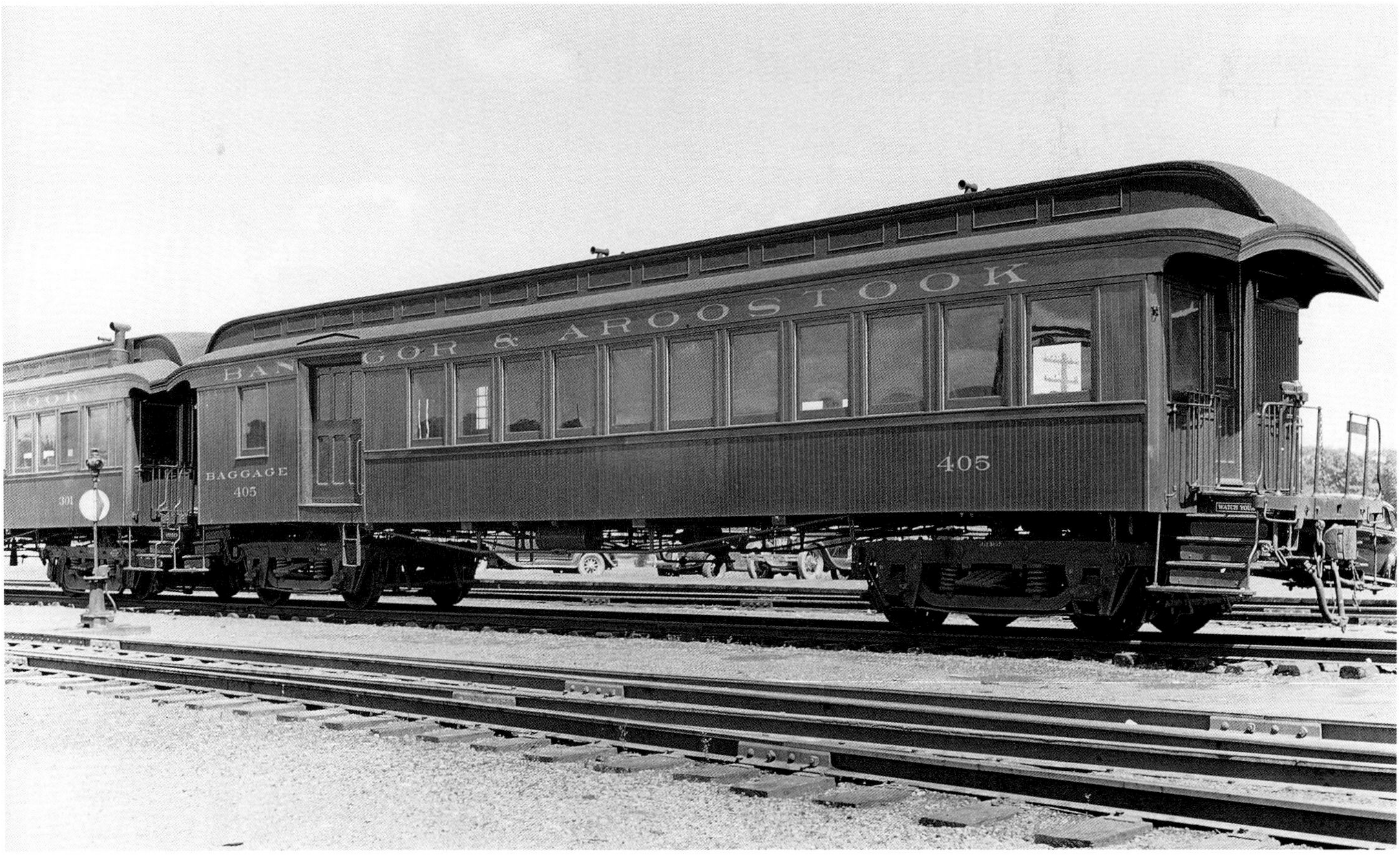
BANGOR & AROOSTOOK
BAGGAGE
405
405

Open-platform baggage-coach #406 seating thirty-eight passengers waited with other passenger cars at Van Buren, Maine, in July 1937. The side windows had fancy rounded upper panes and one window per side was provided in the baggage section. Roller bearings had been applied to the vintage drop-equalized trucks. A steel center sill in the truss-rod underframe kept this car in operation into the 1940s. High mounted switch stands were normal for locations with heavy snowfall during the winter months.

Combine #408 was similar to #406, but no window was provided in the baggage section. The carbody with a truss-rod underframe rode on four-wheel drop-equalized trucks. Seating in the coach section accommodated thirty-eight passengers and the single door per side baggage section took up the remaining space in the carbody. BAR #408 was at Derby Shops in July 1935.

In storage at Derby Shops in July 1935 was center combine #450. Converted from an all-coach, #450 had a center baggage section built in the car with a single baggage door per side. Coal stoves provided heating for both passenger sections and the center baggage room. The open-platform car had truss rods and four-wheel trucks.

Another homemade center combine seating forty-eight passengers was #451, also photographed at Derby Shops in July 1935. With carbody windows similar to #406, it had a baggage section added to the center of the carbody, but the baggage door was placed for some reason off-center. With a center sill applied during the 1920s, the truss-rod underframe still remained at the outside positions.

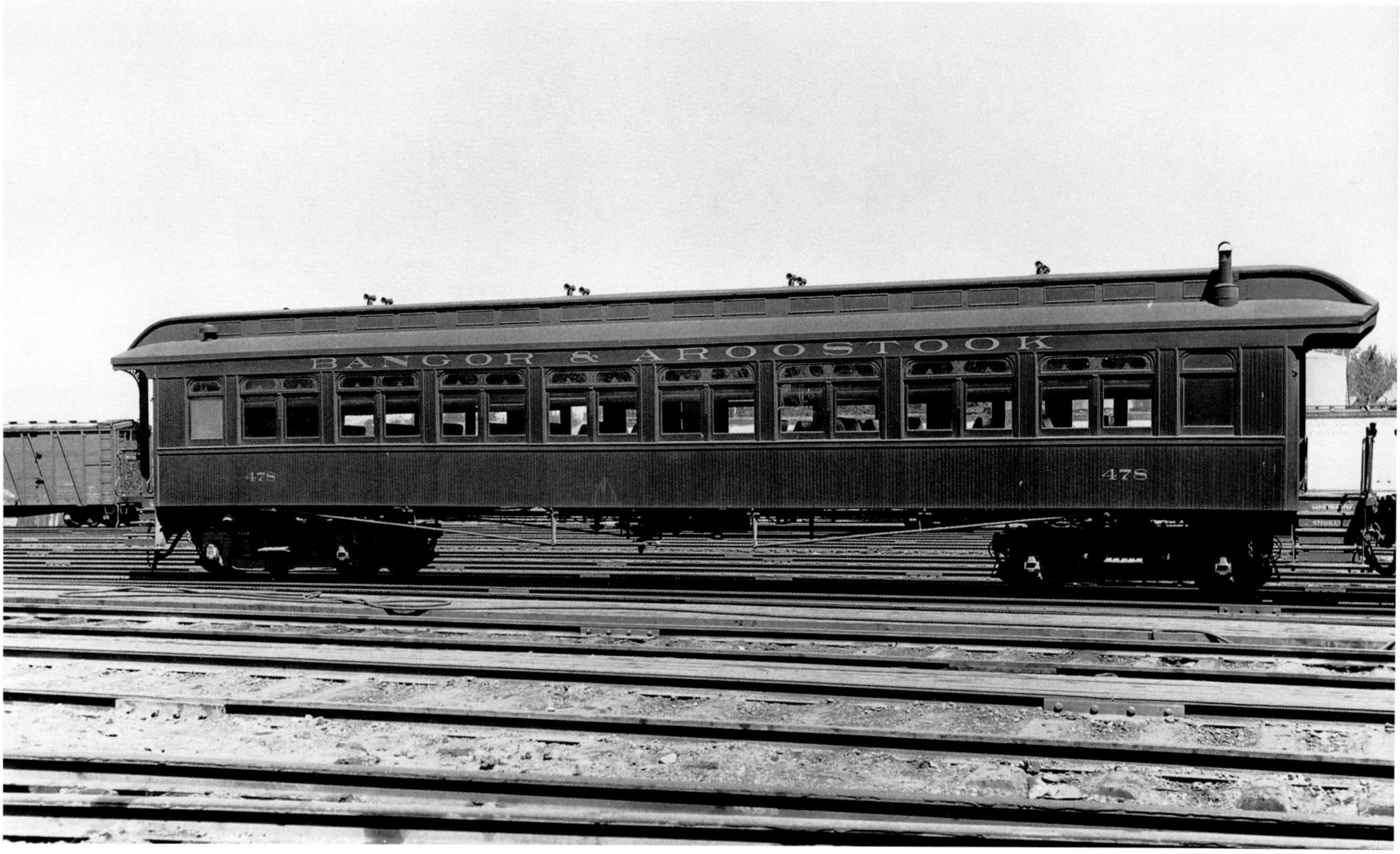
BANGOR & AROOSTOOK
478
478

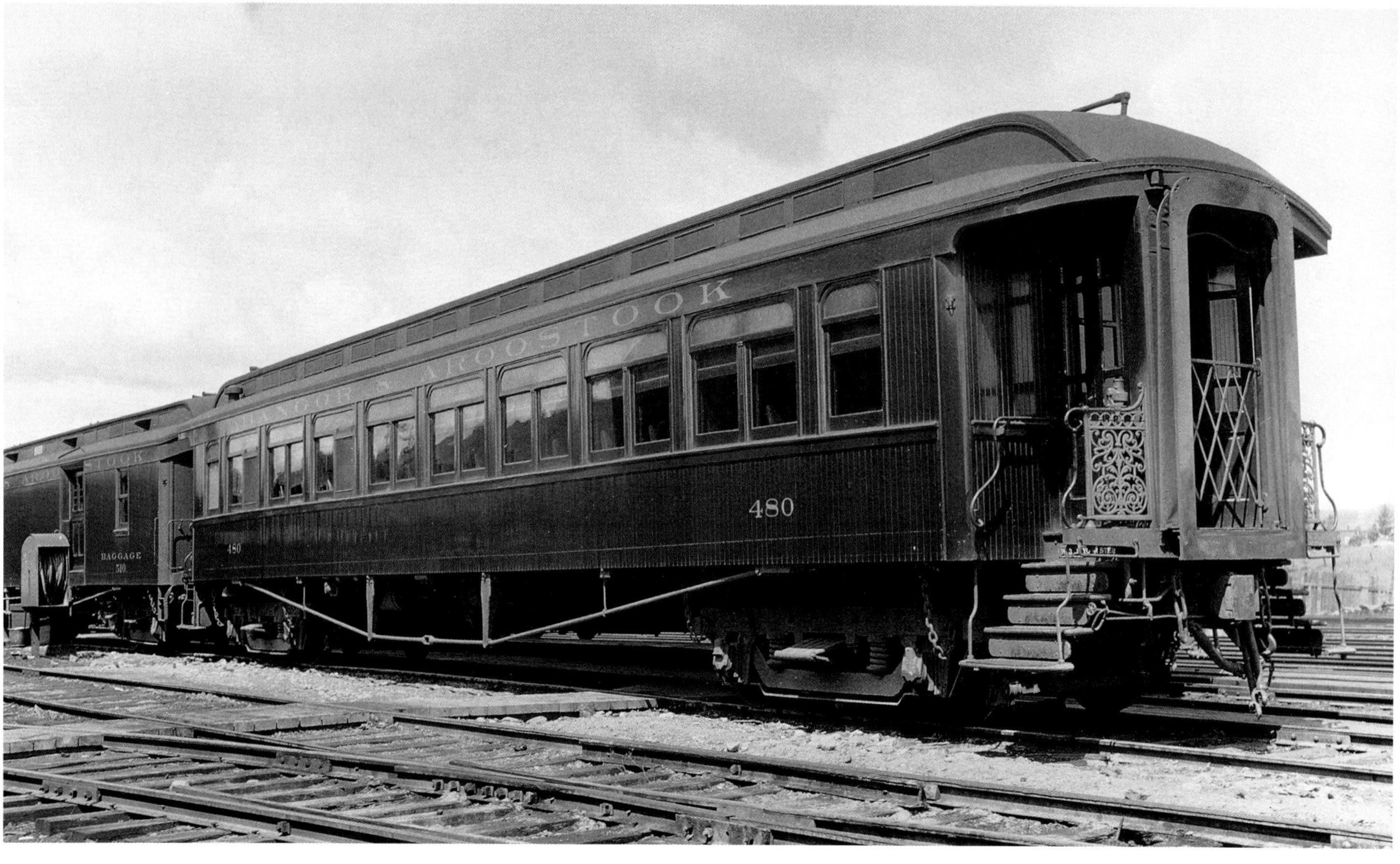
480
480
BAGGAGE
510

With a narrow vestibule on one end and an open platform on the other end, coach #478 was positioned at Van Buren, Maine, in July 1937. Fancy upper panes in the windows still were in place in this mid-1930s scene. One end of the car housed a bathroom and the other end a coal stove. The center double windows allowed seating for thirty-two on each side. Truss rods and a steel center sill supported the weight of the wooden carbody. This car seated sixty passengers.

Another Van Buren car in July 1937 was coach #480. The end view displayed the closed vestibule gate, closed narrow vestibule doors and the fancy cast-iron grills on either side of the vestibule. Across the roof was the electrical wiring for the lighting system installed after the car was built. Truss rods were only at outside edge of the carbody and the center supported by a steel center sill. Seating was provided for sixty-eight passengers.

Before the arrival of "American Flyer" coaches, BAR's fleet of coaches were all wooden. The view at Bangor Station on July 17, 1935, showed an entirely wooden fleet of BAR passenger equipment. BAR #482 was one of the road's "newer" passenger cars with a steel center sill and truss rods. The wooden carbody ended in a narrow vestibule with the outside end door open.

# BAGGAGE CARS

Like baggage car #502, car #501 had open platforms at both ends, two side-doors and one window for the agent. The cast-steel drop-equalized trucks had a top recess to clear the body bolster. Electrical equipment had been installed, two battery boxes between the sliding doors and an axle generator belt, driven off the front truck. Number 501 was positioned with #503 at Van Buren, Maine, in July 1937.

Wooden baggage car #502 had a steel underframe and drop-equalizer four-wheel trucks. This open platform baggage car had two side doors per side plus one window between the doors for additional lighting for the baggage man. Baggage #502 was at Derby passenger station in July 1935.

Baggage car #507 at Boston's North Station passenger yard in July 1937 was actually in intercity service. The car had a steel underframe, battery boxes for lighting and two-inch steam connectors at each end. The large baggage door was on the Railway Express end of the car and the smaller door plus two windows in the section for baggage-service bags and boxes. The car had narrow vestibule ends, but the doors had been removed. Overall length of the car was sixty-six foot six-inches. Wooden baggage cars 506 - 508 with steel underframes lasted on the BAR into the early 1950s.

Coupled to coach #480, baggage car #510 was positioned at the station platform at Van Buren, Maine, in July 1937. With two side doors and two end side windows, #510 was equipped for an agent to handle Railway Express packages. Viewed from the B end, the hand brake worked the B end truck through a vertical chain and bell crank arrangement.

# RPO-BAGGAGE

Built in 1946, BAR #531 was an all-steel baggage car with two 6 foot and two 8 foot side doors, a one-of-a-kind on the BAR. With a weight of 112,500 pounds, this car measured 73 foot 7 inches over buffers. Its 6' x 11' four-wheel trucks had 36 inch wheels with trucks set on 54 foot 9 inch truck centers. Number 531 was captured on film at Van Buren, Maine, on July 19, 1952.

Unique to the Bangor & Aroostook were four "American Flyer" RPO-baggage cars. Under lot W6520, the Osgood-Bradley Plant of Pullman-Standard assembled three, #566-568, RPO-baggage cars in October 1937. Riding on 41-E trucks, the cars had a standard fifteen-foot postal section and two sliding doors per side in the baggage section. Each car had four 5 foot 6 inch side doors. The fourth car, #569, joined the BAR fleet in June 1938, built to the same specification, under lot W6560. Parked next to the turntable, #568 was at Van Buren, Maine, on July 19, 1952, still painted in the dark green painting arrangement. Sold to the Maine Central in 1961, #568 became MEC #356.

# WORK CARS

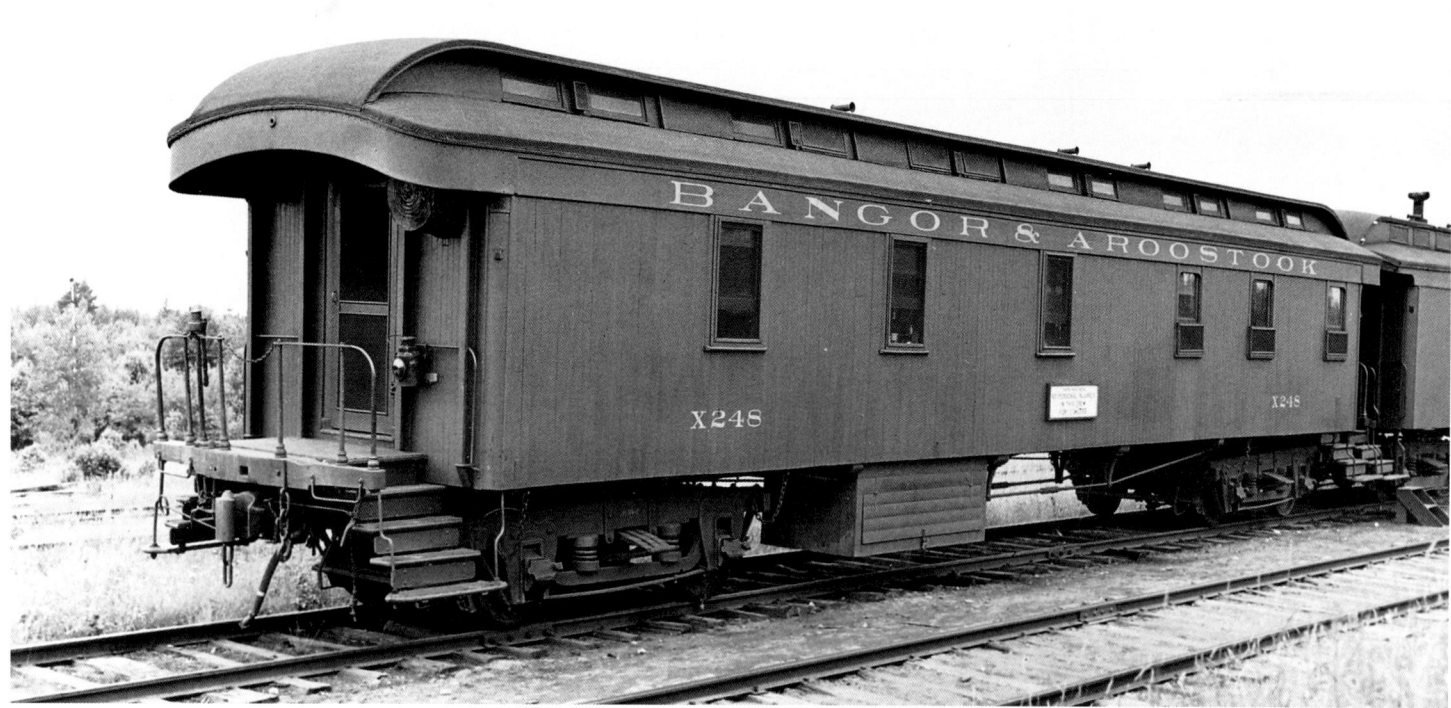

Former baggage car, now in non-revenue service, #X242 was at Van Buren, Maine, coupled to a wheel car. The wooden open-platform work car had one door plus two windows per side. The four-wheel drop-equalized trucks were of wood and steel construction. Windows along the roofline provided additional lighting for the interior.

At La Grange, Maine, on July 17, 1935, camp car, former coach, #X248 rested on July 17, 1935. The side windows had been reduced to six per side when equipped as a camp car. With a wooden carbody, the car rode on steel/wood drop-equalized trucks with cast iron wheels.

After retirement from passenger service, #X259 was converted from a 300-series coach. Stored at Derby, Maine, on January 11, 1965, #X259 had been repainted red with a black underframe and trucks. The outside window arrangement remained the same as when the coach was in revenue service.

Painted in the gray and blue work equipment color scheme, work-observation #X1206 was at Searsport, Maine, on August 8, 1959. The six-wheel truck truss-rod observation came from the #194-196 group parlor-café cars. These six-wheel trucks were of the Pullman 2410 design with plain bearings on each axle.

# INTRODUCTION

## Maine Central Passenger Equipment

The Maine Central Railroad Company operated a 981-mile railroad mostly within the state of Maine. In the 1930s and 1940s, the MEC was locally owned, but operated by the Boston & Maine management under contract. By 1950, the passenger revenues were $1,605,684 with a combined passenger and freight operation ratio of 77.58. Passenger equipment included forty-four coaches, thirteen combination baggage-coaches, two parlor cars, two club cars, fifteen postal cars and forty-nine other head-end cars.

Our review of Maine Central passenger cars starts in the 1920s when all-steel coaches were replacing the wooden car fleet. At that time the Maine Central was operated by a Boston & Maine management team, all purchases for new cars made through the Boston office. In order to obtain the best pricing, often MEC cars were purchased at the same time as B&M cars using a common design. Maine Central was also one of the New England railroads that favored Osgood-Bradley of Worcester, Massachusetts, as the car builder of choice.

In 1921, the MEC purchased baggage-mail cars #415-416 from Osgood-Bradley with a thirty-foot mail section and a thirty-foot baggage section. These all-steel cars rode on four-wheel Standard trucks. At the same time, Osgood-Bradley furnished sixty-four-foot long baggage cars #328-334. These cars had two five-foot six-inch sliding doors per side, UC brake equipment and four-wheel Standard trucks. More all-steel mail cars were added to the fleet, #361-367, in 1923, only this time the cars had a fifteen-foot mail section and a forty-five foot baggage compartment. These cars also had four-wheel Standard trucks.

For 1924, the MEC purchased all-steel Osgood-Bradley coaches #213-221. Originally numbered #183-191, some cars had seating for sixty-six plus ten in the smoking section (cars #213-216 & 220-221) while #217-219 had seating for seventy in the coach section and ten in the smoking section. Also purchased were baggage-mail cars #417-420 from Osgood-Bradley having a thirty-foot mail section. Both the coaches and mail cars rode on four-wheel Standard trucks. In 1928, the MEC went back to Osgood-Bradley for two more baggage-mail cars #368 and 369. They were of the same design as the #361-367 group with a forty-five foot baggage section and a fifteen-foot mail section.

The last cars ordered at the start of the Great Depression were coaches #261-265 and passenger-baggage cars #521-522 from Osgood-Bradley in 1931. This was a joint order with the Boston & Maine as the B&M purchased coaches #4581-4584 and combines #3608-3609. Both the B&M and MEC cars rode on Commonwealth, four-wheel, SKF roller-bearing trucks. The coaches had "bucket" seats for sixty-eight passengers and the combines seating for forty-four. In 1950, B&M #4581 joined the MEC roster as #266 replacing #264 that the B&M had wrecked at Biddeford, Maine, on March 26, 1950. Gold leaf lettering five inches high spelled out MAINE CENTRAL at the center line beneath the belt rail of the car followed by five inch numbers centered four inches below the road name on a Pullman green carbody. In conjunction with the B&M, the carbody color changed to Tuscan red in November 1941 and maroon in August 1949. Under the Tuscan red and maroon painting arrangements, the step risers and treads, side and end handholds were painted black.

B&M's Budd-built FLYING YANKEE three-unit stainless-steel train of 1935 did operate on the Boston-Portland-Bangor route, but the MEC did not purchase a twin train. In 1935 and again in 1937, the B&M ordered "American Flyer" styled lightweight coaches, but the MEC did not have an "add-on" order for these cars. Maine Central's first lightweight passenger equipment was not ordered until November 1945, when it pooled with the B&M for a twenty-four-car order to Pullman - Standard's Osgood-Bradley plant. MEC's half of the order included restaurant-lounge cars #15-16, coaches #240-247 and combines #540-541, all with names. The coach-smokers provided fifty-six seats in Heywood-Wakefield's "sleepy hollow" seating in the coach section and seating for ten in the smoking lounge. Each of the two restaurant-lounge cars provided twenty-four seats in the diner and eighteen in the lounge. The combines had an almost thirty-foot baggage room with one six-foot wide sliding door on each side, a smoking lounge for eight and a coach section seating thirty-six. The vestibule end provided space for the men's and women's wash and toilet rooms. All cars rode on 41-NP trucks with a combination of helical and elliptical springs. First of the group to leave were the two restaurant-lounge cars sold to the Chicago and Eastern Illinois Railroad in 1951 and MEC coaches were sold to the Missouri Pacific in 1960.

# Maine Central Passenger Equipment Roster 1930 - 1960 (cars built after 1900)

| Car No. | Type | Builders | Year Built |
|---|---|---|---|
| 15 - 16 | Restaurant-Lounge | PS/Bradley | 1947 |
| 23 - 30 | Coach | Pullman | 1906 |
| 31 - 40 | Coach | MEC | 1901 - 04 |
| 41 - 42 | Coach | Wason | 1906 |
| 58 - 59 | Coach - smoker | MEC | 1903 |
| 81 | Baggage | Pullman | 1907 |
| 82 - 83 | Horse - baggage | Pullman | 1905 |
| 84 | Baggage | MEC | 1905 |
| 85 - 86 | Baggage | Pullman | 1906 |
| 87 - 88 | Baggage | Laconia | 1908 - 09 |
| 151 - 154 | Coach | Pullman | 1908 |
| 155 - 168 | Coach | Laconia | 1910 - 11 |
| 170 - 174 | Coach | Bradley | 1912 |
| 201 - 212 | Coach | Pullman | 1914 - 17 |
| 213 - 221 | Coach | Bradley | 1924 |
| 240 - 247 | Coach | PS/Bradley | 1947 |
| 261 - 265 | Coach | Bradley | 1931 |
| 266 (ex B&M 4581) | Coach | Bradley | 1931 |
| 291 | Baggage | MEC | 1903 |
| 301 - 304 | Baggage | Pullman | 1908 |
| 305 - 306 | Baggage | MEC | 1918 - 19 |
| 307 | Baggage | Laconia | 1911 |
| 308 | Baggage | MEC | 1919 |
| 309 | Baggage | Laconia | 1911 |
| 310 | Baggage | Bradley | 1912 |
| 311 - 313 | Baggage | MEC | 1903 - 04 |
| 314 - 316 | Baggage | Laconia | 1910 - 11 |
| 317 - 319 | Baggage | Pullman | 1905 - 06 |
| 320 - 323 | Baggage | Laconia | 1910 - 14 |
| 324 - 327 | Baggage | Pullman | 1914 - 17 |
| 328 - 334 | Baggage | Bradley | 1921 |
| 340 - 341 | Horse - baggage | Wason | 1906 |
| 361 - 367 | Baggage - Mail | Bradley | 1923 |
| 368 - 369 | Baggage - Mail | Bradley | 1928 |
| 405 - 41 | Baggage - Mail | Bradley | 1912 |
| 411 - 412 | Baggage - Mail | Laconia | 1914 |
| 413 - 414 | Baggage - Mail | Pullman | 1914 |
| 415 - 416 | Baggage - Mail | Bradley | 1921 |
| 417 - 420 | Baggage - Mail | Bradley | 1924 |
| 452 | Baggage - smoker | MEC | 1903 |
| 453 | Baggage - smoker | Laconia | 1905 |
| 501 - 503 | Baggage - smoker | Laconia | 1910 |
| 504 and 507 | Smoker | Pullman | 1905 |
| 505 - 506 and 508 | Baggage - smoker | Pullman | 1905 |
| 509 - 510 | Baggage - smoker | Laconia | 1909 |
| 521 - 522 | Baggage - passenger | Bradley | 1931 |
| 540 - 541 | Baggage - passenger | PS/Bradley | 1947 |
| 608 - 611 | Mail | Laconia | 1914 |
| 612 | Mail | Pullman | 1917 |
| 1200 - 1203 | Diner | Pullman | 1906 - 07 |

# WOODEN COACHES

Maine Central coach #26 was built by the Pullman Company in 1906. MEC coaches #23-30 were all built at the same time with an inside length of 56 feet7 inches seating 76 passengers and equipped with oil lights. These open platform cars rode on standard Pullman 4-wheel trucks and had a truss rod underframe. Stored, MEC #26 was photographed at Brunswick, Maine, in July 1935.

MEC coach #37 was built by the Maine Central in 1902 with oil lights. Coaches #34-37 formed the 1902 group of MEC-built open-platform coaches, all 56 feet 7 inches in inside length and constructed with a wood underframe. Seating capacity for #37 was 68 and the car was equipped with a Vapor Heating System. Photographed on July 16, 1935, on a siding near the Bangor Station, #37 had been removed from revenue passenger service.

Maine Central wooden coach #138 sat in the storage line at Brunswick, Maine, in July 1935. This semi-closed vestibule coach had a truss-rod underframe and four-wheel drop-equalized trucks. Each side had eight paired windows plus three single windows with a fancy trim between each window. The cast iron grillwork remained at each end mounted on top of the end sill with lettering on the steps indicating that the cars were in storage.

Coach #155 was built by the Laconia Car Company in 1910 with an inside length of 61 feet 4 inches and seating eighty-seven passengers. The car rode on Pullman four-wheel trucks and came with a steel underframe. In 1947, coach #155 was rebuilt to work car #935. On July 18, 1935, coach #155 was positioned in front of the Lewistown, Maine, Station.

In 1911, Laconia Car Company built eight, #161-168, wooden, steel underframe, full vestibule coaches for the MEC with an inside length of 67 feet 2 inches and equipped with gas lights and a Vapor heating system. Riding on Standard 4-wheel trucks, the coaches had seating for 87 passengers. On a hot summer day in July 1935, #166 plus several others waited on a siding at Old Orchard Beach, Maine, for a passenger extra.

Laconia Car Company built coaches #161-168 in 1911 having an inside length of 67 feet 2 inches and seating eighty-seven passengers. These cars with a steel underframe rode on Standard four-wheel trucks. As built, the cars had a Vapor heating system and gaslights. In 1946, coach #168 was rebuilt to work car #922, a cook-office-diner and finally retired on October 7, 1963. On July 17, 1935, coach #168 was coupled to a string of passenger cars at Waterville, Maine.

# STEEL COACHES

Maine Central #212 was originally built as MEC #255 by the Pullman Company in 1917 with an inside length of 67 feet 3 inches. Seating eighty-seven, the car had electric lighting and rode on Standard four-wheel drop-equalized trucks. With its upper sash stained glass windows still in place, #212 was photographed at Portland Station on June 3, 1952.

Osgood-Bradley built the MEC #183-191 group of coaches in 1924 with an inside length of 70 feet 3 inches. These all-steel cars were renumbered 213-221 and placed in main line service. Car #213 had seating for seventy-seven passengers, sixty-six in the coach section and eleven in the smoking section. Number 213 was photographed at Boston in 1955.

All-steel coach #214 (originally #184) was built by Osgood-Bradley in 1924, part of the group #183-191. Seating seventy-seven, sixty-six in the coach section and eleven in the smoking section, the inside length of the car was 70 feet 3 inches. Each car had Standard four-wheel trucks, but the seating arrangement was different in some of these cars. Car #214 had an electric lighting system and a Vapor heating system. In joint B&M/MEC service, coach #214 waited at North Station coupled to a Pullman.

In 1931 Osgood-Bradley built five all-steel coaches for the Maine Central. These 71 feet 6 inch long inside length cars rode on Commonwealth four-wheel trucks equipped with SKF roller bearings. At the same time, Osgood-Bradley built four duplicate, #4581-4584, coaches for the Boston & Maine. Each car seated sixty-eight passengers, had a Vapor steam heating system and was equipped with electric lights. Each car had a Westinghouse UC air brake system with an 18 x 12 body mounted air brake cylinder. In front of the Bangor Station, coach #263 stopped for its next assignment on July 20, 1952.

After World War II, the B&M and MEC placed an order with Pullman-Standard's Osgood-Bradley plant in Worcester to build twenty-four passenger cars. Within the order were eight coaches, #240-247, for the Maine Central. Each car had seats with adjustable footrests, roomy smoking lounges and toilets. The equipment went into service on the FLYING YANKEE, PINE TREE and KENNEBEC between Boston-Portland-Bangor. Coach #244, the SAGADAHOC, was photographed at Bangor, Maine, on July 20, 1952 about five years after delivery.

MEC's coach ABENAKI was photographed at Bangor, Maine, on July 20, 1952. Car names were picked by grammar school children located along the Portland-Bangor route. These Pullman-Standard cars were equipped with "Sleepy Hollow" seats, picture windows, air-conditioning and fluorescent lighting. Built in Worcester, Massachusetts, by Osgood-Bradley (lot W6778, plan W46352), coaches #240-247 were delivered in 1947 for joint service with the B&M. Also included in the order were restaurant-lounge cars #15-16 and combines #540-541. At the end of MEC passenger service, those twelve cars were sold to the Chicago & Eastern Illinois Railroad.

Volume 2   Bangor & Aroostook / Maine Central

# RPO-BAGGAGE

Maine Central #362 was built by Osgood-Bradley in 1923, part of the #361-367 group of baggage-mail cars. With an overall length of sixty-four feet eight inches, the car had a 15-foot mail section and a 45-foot baggage section. Trucks were of the four-wheel Standard drop-equalized design. RPO-baggage #362 was photographed at Portland, Maine, on June 8, 1952. (J. Emmons Lancaster Collection)

MEC #408 arrived on the property in 1912 from Osgood-Bradley, part of the #405-410 group with steel underframes and a wooden carbody. Each car had a 30-foot mail section and a 29 foot 10 inch baggage section. The car rode on Standard four-wheeled drop-equalized trucks. Later #408 became non-revenue work car #928.

In 1921, the MEC purchased two RPO-baggage cars numbered #415-416. Each car had a 30-foot mail section and 30-foot baggage section with two sliding doors per side. This 64-foot 2-inch long car over buffers rode on Standard four-wheel drop-equalized trucks and had two ceiling fans in the RPO section. Number 415 was photographed at the Portland Station on June 8, 1952. (J. Emmons Lancaster Collection)

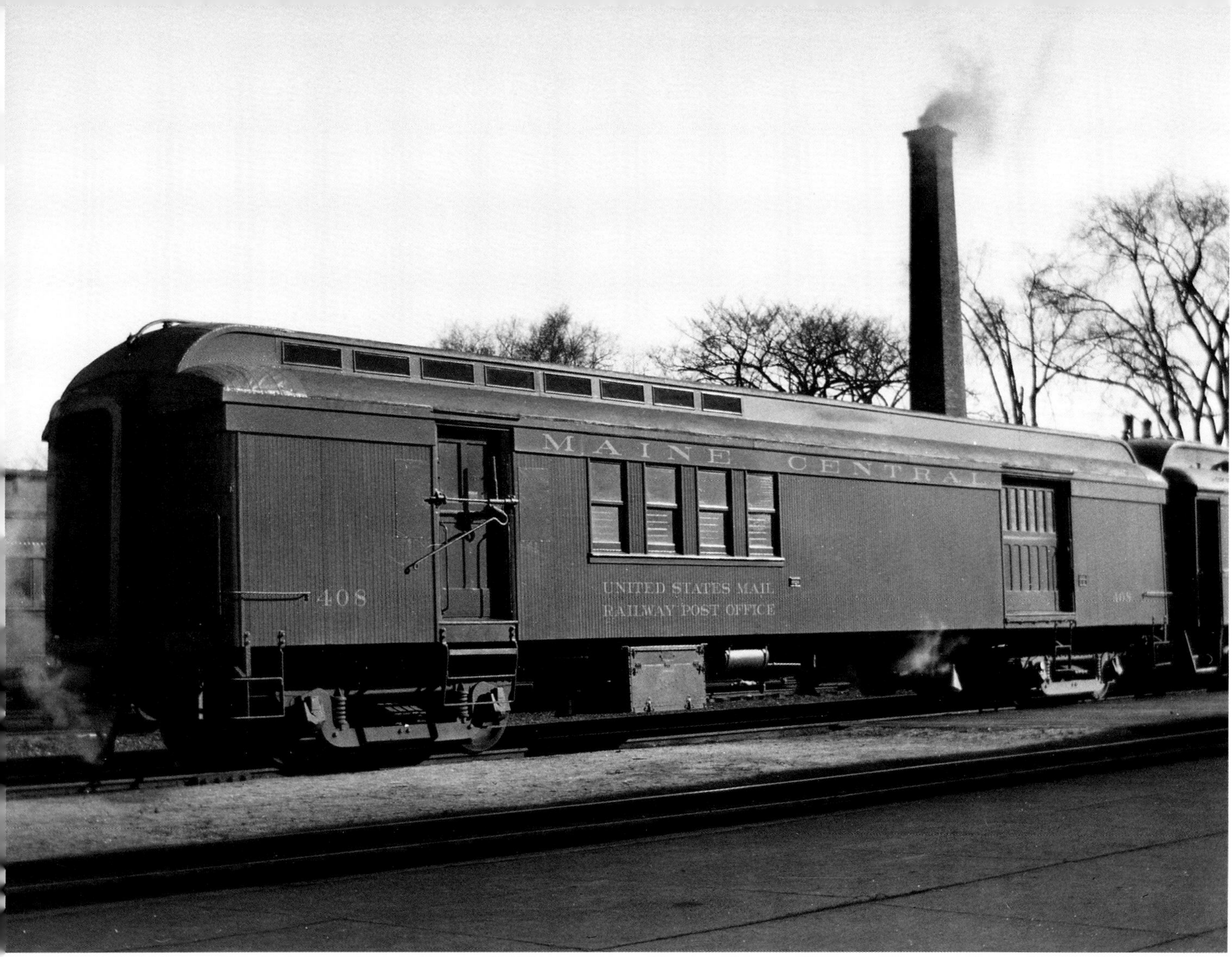
MAINE CENTRAL
408
UNITED STATES MAIL
RAILWAY POST OFFICE

MAINE CENTRAL
415
UNITED STATES MAIL
RAILWAY POST OFFICE

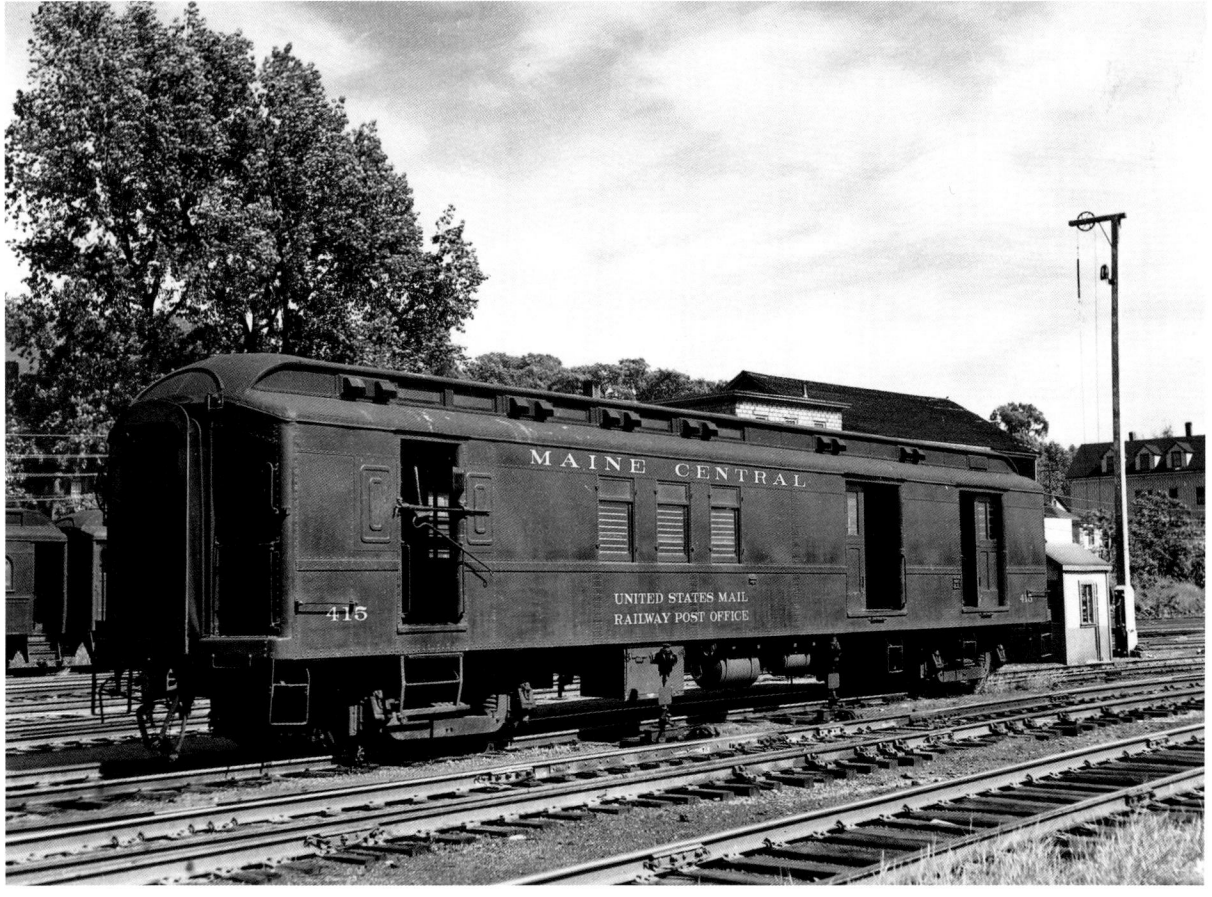

Wason built two horse-baggage cars, #325-326 (later #340-341), for the MEC in 1906 riding on Standard four-wheel drop-equalized trucks. As originally built, each car had fifteen stalls for horses and the car measured 65 foot 5 inches over buffers. Both of these steel underframe, wooden carbody cars were retired in August 1958, many years after the April 1939 photograph in Bath, Maine.

# COMBINES

Also in storage at Brunswick, Maine, was wooden combine #428 with twin sliding doors on each side. Passengers could be seated, sixteen per side, behind the paired windows with a stove behind the single window. The wooden carbody rode on four-wheel drop-equalized trucks and the car had a truss-rod underframe. The design of the coach section was similar to coach #138.

Wooden combine #501 was built by the Laconia Car Company in 1910 seating forty-eight in the passenger smoking section. Combines #501-503 were built as a group, riding on CP-4 four-wheel trucks with a passenger section measuring 39 feet long and baggage section 21 feet 3 inches long. When originally built, these three cars were numbered 211-213 and equipped with two coal stoves and gaslights. The baggage door opening was six foot, one door per side.

During MEC's program to replace wooden passenger cars, the road purchased from Osgood-Bradley Car Company two all-steel combination passenger-baggage cars #521-522 in 1931. The inside length of the baggage section was 30 feet 3 inches and the 44-seat passenger section 44 feet 5 inches. A blind end formed the baggage section and a vestibule provided entrance at the passenger end. The Commonwealth 4-wheel trucks were equipped with SKF roller bearings. Both #521-522 had electric lights and a Vapor steam heating system. Photographed at North Station on July 4, 1936, #522 headed the passenger consist for a Portland-bound train. The car became rider car #322 and used with observation car #333 on special trains. It later had a steam generator installed in the baggage section.

Built in 1947 by Pullman - Standard at the Osgood-Bradley Plant in Worcester, Massachusetts, were two steel combines, #540 and 541, for the Maine Central and two, #3800 and 3801, delivered to the B&M. Car #541 was named FOREST QUEEN and its twin, #540, named LUMBER KING. Each car had an almost 30-foot long baggage section with one 6-foot wide sliding door on each side, a smoking lounge for eight passengers and a coach section seating thirty-six in "Sleepy Hollow" seats. The handbrake end of the car was the "B" end. These cars were built under Pullman plan 46353, lot 6778 and went into the passenger train consists for the FLYING YANKEE, PINE TREE and KENNEBEC, operating between Boston-Portland and Bangor. On July 18, 1952, #541 waited at North Station for a Portland-bound train.

# MOTOR COACHES

# WORK CARS

MEC steam generator car #111 was used for many years at the Bangor Roundhouse. Originally built as coach #178 in 1914, later #204, it became a portable heating car for the MEC in 1955 and its painting arrangement of green with yellow stripes matched the MEC E-7 diesel passenger units. The car rode on six-wheel Standard trucks and measured 77 feet 1 inch over buffers. (Russ Monroe Collection)

Maine Central Transportation Company motor coach #604 waited for passengers in 1940. This thirty-seven passenger ACF bus indicated Bangor in the roll sign, but the street sign indicated a bus for Skowhegan, Madison, and Bingham. During the 1940s, Maine Central substitute motor coach transportation for the branch line passenger trains. This bus service ran between Waterville-Skowhegan-Madison and Bingham, connecting at Waterville with main line passenger trains. (J. Emmons Lancaster Collection)

About 1940, motor coach #608 stopped to pick up passengers for Lewiston. Coach #608 was an ACF bus model seating thirty-seven passengers. During the 1940s and 1950s, the MEC operated extensive bus service between Lewiston-Brunswick-Bath, and Portland-Brunswick-Bath-Rockland. (J. Emmons Lancaster Collection)

Maine Central work car #919 was a former RPO-baggage car with open platforms at both ends. The baggage section had two side doors, one large and one small, per side plus a small door and large door in the postal section. Now numbered 919, the car waited in a work train at Brunswick, Maine, on July 15, 1935. The car had a truss-rod underframe and rode on four-wheel drop-equalized trucks.

Originally built as B&M coach #538 by the Laconia Car Company in 1911, this coach became MEC work car #957 in 1950. The car was redesigned as a washroom-recreation-sleeper for a camp train and could sleep twelve men. With a steel underframe, the car had a lightweight of 85,100 pounds. Work coach #957 was at Waterville, Maine, on July 23, 1968.

MEC #1339, a former baggage car, now belonged to a work train at Brunswick, Maine, in July 1935. Each side had three baggage doors, a truss-rod underframe and open-end platforms. The car rode on four-wheel drop-equalized trucks and now served as a tool and storage car in non-revenue service.

Also in the work train at Brunswick, Maine, in July 1935 was work coach #1379. It also was an open-platform car with a truss-rod underframe and four-wheel drop-equalized trucks. This non-revenue camp car was heated by coal stoves and equipped as living quarters for an M of W gang. All of the nine paired windows plus a single window were in place.

# OFFICE CARS

Originally built as office car NITUNA, car #333 was photographed at Portland, Maine, on September 21, 1957. The car measured 83 feet, 7 and three-quarter inches over couplers and had four private rooms. Built in 1924 by the Pullman Company, the car was painted dark green with yellow lettering and a yellow bottom stripe. This all-steel car had UC brake equipment with two 16 x 12 inch cylinders and carried a weight of 182,300 pounds including trucks. (Russ Monroe Collection)

# INDEX

**A**
"American Flyer" .........................................2, 3, 6, 14, 21, 25, 28
Aroostook Flyer ..............................................................3
**B**
Bangor, Maine......................9, 10, 12, 15, 21, 28, 31, 36, 43, 45
Bath, Maine ..................................................................40
Biddeford, Maine ............................................................28
Boston, Massachusetts................................3, 24, 28, 35, 36, 43
Boston & Maine ...................................3, 28, 35, 36, 43, 46
Brunswick, Maine ............................................31, 41, 45, 46, 47
**C**
Canadian National..............................................................3
Caribou, Maine ......................................................6, 11, 16
Chicago and Eastern Illinois ................................................28
Commonwealth ....................................................28, 36, 43
**D**
Derby, Maine....................................5, 6, 8, 11, 12, 18, 19, 23, 27
**F**
"Flying Yankee"............................................................28, 36, 43
**G**
Gull ..............................................................................3
**K**
"Kennebec" ..............................................................36, 43
**L**
Laconia Car Company ..............................................2, 33, 43, 46

La Grange, Maine ..............................................................26
Lewistown, Maine ..............................................................33
**M**
Madawaska, Maine ............................................................16
**N**
New Haven ..................................................................3, 16
North Station ........................................................24, 35, 43
**O**
Old Orchard Beach, Maine ..................................................33
Ontario Northland ..............................................................3
Osgood-Bradley ..................3, 6, 16, 25, 28, 35, 36, 38, 43
**P**
"Pine Tree" ..............................................................36, 43
Portland, Maine ......................................28, 35, 36, 38, 43, 45
Potatoland ......................................................................3
Pullman Company..................2, 3, 5, 6, 7, 27, 28, 31, 33, 35, 43
Pullman-Standard ..................................3, 6, 16, 25, 28, 36, 43
**S**
Searsport, Maine ..............................................................27
SKF ..................................................................28, 36, 43
**V**
Van Buren, Maine ..............3, 7, 8, 10, 15, 18, 21, 22, 24, 25, 26
**W**
Waterville, Maine ....................................................33, 45, 46
Worcester, Massachusetts ....................................3, 16, 28, 36, 43